AF479931

Little Bear
and
Singing Bird
Written by Anna Park
Illustrated by Sabdo Purnomo

Little Bear and Singing Bird

Anna Park

illustrations by Sabdo Purnomo

In a cave near the dark forest,
there lived Little Bear,
who had no friends.

Little Bear was lonely.
One day, while walking through the forest,
she saw Singing Bird in a tree.
Maybe Singing Bird could be her friend?

"Hi, Singing Bird. You are so high up in the tree. What can you see from there?" Little Bear asked.

Singing Bird smiled at Little Bear but did not speak.

Little Bear felt ignored because Singing Bird did not answer. But she was happy that Singing Bird had smiled at her.

The next day, Little Bear returned to the same spot and saw Singing Bird again, sitting in the same tree.

"Good morning, Singing Bird. Can I visit you every morning and talk to you? I would love to be your friend."

Again, Singing Bird smiled at her but did not speak.

'Why does he not answer?'
Little Bear wondered.

Little Bear came to visit Singing Bird every day for the next week. Little Bear always greeted Singing Bird and asked a question.

Singing Bird never spoke.

But he always smiled when he saw Little Bear.

One night in her cave, Little Bear couldn't sleep.
She kept thinking about Singing Bird.
Why didn't he speak to her?

Then Little Bear heard
something outside.
It sounded like a
bird singing.

Little Bear walked
out of the cave and
saw Singing Bird.

"Little Bear, I love that you come to see me.
Your visit keeps me happy throughout the day.
I can see so much from up here, and I love living in the tree.
But you live down there in the cave,
so I am afraid we can't be friends."

Little Bear was happy to hear Singing Bird. But she felt sad again when Singing Bird stopped singing.

"So we can't be friends...?" Little Bear shook her head sadly in disappointment.

Brokenhearted, Little Bear went back into her cave and did not come out for days.

Singing Bird waited for Little Bear to visit. But Little Bear never came. Singing Bird missed Little Bear.

One night, Singing Bird came back to the cave and sang again.

"Little Bear, Little Bear, I miss you talking to me every morning. I am sorry I pushed you away. I want you back, Little Bear. I will wait here for you until the sun comes up."

Little Bear heard
Singing Bird, but she was scared that Singing
Bird would push her away again, so she
did not go out to see Singing Bird.

Singing Bird waited until sunrise. He finally
felt ready to talk to Little Bear and was
disappointed that Little Bear didn't come.

A few days later,
Little Bear decided to go
for a walk. She passed by the tree,
but Singing Bird was not there.

The next day, Little Bear went for a walk
again, and Singing Bird was still not there.

That night, Singing Bird came
back to the cave and sang.

"Little Bear, while I was gone for a few days,
I realized that it's hard to meet a friend like you.
And I want you back. When you come,
I will tell you everything I see up here,
and you can tell me everything you see in the cave."

Little Bear heard Singing Bird's
song. She walked out of the
cave and saw Singing Bird.

And they finally started talking.
They talked and talked for
hours… until dawn.

Looking at the sunrise, Singing Bird asked,
"Little Bear, will you be my friend?"

Little Bear answered, "Singing Bird, I think we've been friends for a while now without realizing it. Even though you were only singing, you were singing the answers to my questions. I am happy to be your friend, always."

Happily, Singing Bird flew down to
Little Bear and sat on her shoulder.

They continued talking as
they moved toward the sun.

To my children, Olivia, Aiden, and Ethan,
who have become new friends with Little Bear in recent years.
Thank you for flying down to Little Bear's shoulder.
To my best friend and now husband, Shawn. I love you always.
And lastly, to the Singing Bird who inspired me to write this book.
I hope you keep singing for as long as you can breathe.
Just like you said you would.

A. P.